Sunken Secrets

Wikitude is a world

application, provide

location.

Through Wikitude you will be able to
access the information in this booklet
via a mobile phone or device.

To use the Wikitude application
(www.wikitude.org) you need a
phone or a device that supports
applications and has access to the internet.
To access the information follow these simple steps:

1. Download and install Wikitude (free) from the Apps
store, Market or Ovi store (see A below).

2. Search for the **Hampshire and Wight Trust for
Maritime Archaeology world.**

3. Add the world to your desktop (see B below) and open it. By
default it will display using the Camera mode (see C below).

4. Browse the 8 different chapters by pressing Menu and
changing to List (see D below) or Map (see E below) mode.
If you're on the West Wight coast, use Camera mode and
simply point your device towards the sea and pan around
until you see the floating HWTMA icons (see C below).

| A | B | C | D | E |

(Please refer to Wikitude for latest updates and changes)

If you want to share your images or experiences of this
guide with others, please visit
www.hwtma.org.uk/sunkensecrets

Cover image: The Smyrna ©Dave Robbins
Back cover image: The Needles

1. Newtown

Public pathway: The Coastal Path

➤ **Directions:** You get the best view over the estuary by walking out to the end of the boardwalk. Follow Public Footpath sign CB9 from the village centre past the church towards the harbour.

🕐 **Wikitude:** Point your device towards the creek, or choose from the list and select **HWTMA 1. Newtown.**

Podcast: Download **Sunken Secrets 1. Newtown.**

Newtown - the Isle of Wight's capital

Newtown, or Francheville as it was previously called, was once the capital of the Isle of Wight, with a flourishing port that has welcomed visitors to the Island for more than 1000 years. The natural bay and estuary provides a sheltered anchorage that has long contributed to the importance of Newtown as a maritime base.

Francheville (Freetown)

The discovery of a stone axe and Neolithic polished flints in the Newtown area is evidence of its long history of use. Newtown is more famous, however, for its flourishing community in the 14th century when more than sixty families lived here. At this time the area boasted a safe harbour, salt works and oyster beds. It was not always so prosperous though; setbacks in Newtown's history include attacks by the Danes in the 11th century and several attacks by the French in the 14th century.

Seal of Newtown (Francheville)

In the 16th century the popularity of Newtown declined. A number of factors are likely to have contributed to this, including French raids, the gradual silting up of the harbour which prevented access by larger vessels, and the increase in free trade at Newport to the east.

Newtown's recent history

The post medieval history of the area is reflected in a fascinating variety of built heritage, including the remains of brick kilns, coastguard cottages and Grade II listed buildings. There are also remains from the 20th century in the form of two bombing decoys, coastal defences and an anti-aircraft battery.

Newtown Creek

Albatross 1905 - A flaming tragedy

The village of Newtown is no longer a major trade and shipping centre, but many ships pass by as they travel along the coast and at the beginning of the 20th century a tragedy occurred just outside the creek.

On the 17th of August 1905 the ship *Albatross* left Thames Haven to make its way to Cardiff with a cargo of 360 barrels of petrol. Due to the nature of the cargo, special safety measures were imposed in port to avoid any fire coming into contact with the wooden barrels containing the petrol. These rules were relaxed when the ship left London: smoking was permitted on board and matches were used to light the ship's lamps. During the journey some of the barrels worked loose in the hold and the hatches had to be removed to secure the barrels. It was also reported that the smell of petrol was so strong that the crew could not sleep below and that traces of oil had been noticed in the water brought up by the bilge pumps.

On August the 23rd the vessel anchored at Ryde Pier during strong winds. By 5pm the wind had moderated and *Albatross* continued its journey. When passing Newtown a loud explosion ripped through the hold, flames shot up from amidships and set the whole ship alight. The crew, who at the time of the explosion had been standing towards the stern of the ship, could not get to the lifeboats because of the flames. Fortunately they were rescued by a boat from a nearby barge called *Vivian*. The ship burned down to the waterline and stranded off Newtown Bay. No remains are visible today.

The tragic loss of the *Albatross* was not unusual for the time and it led to a review of procedures for transporting petrol in wooden barrels that eventually resulted in the practice being abandoned altogether.

2. Bouldnor Cliff

Public pathway: The Coastal Path.

Directions: The Coastal Path takes you through Bouldnor Forest where you can view the bay.

Wikitude: Point your device towards the bay, or choose from the list and select **HWTMA 2. Bouldnor Cliff.**

Podcast: Download **Sunken Secrets 2. Bouldnor Cliff.**

Sunken pre-history
Just offshore, in about 10 metres of water, lies a most magnificent archaeological discovery. Bouldnor Cliff is a Mesolithic site that dates back over 8,000 years. It was discovered in the late 1990s when a diver noticed a lobster excavating

worked flints from the seabed. Since then underwater archaeologists working on the site have recovered a wide range of material including worked wood, flint, hazelnuts and burnt wood.

Archaeologist investigating Bouldnor Cliff

A drowned landscape

Bouldnor Cliff is a drowned landscape which runs parallel to the Isle of Wight's north shore. The site dates from the Mesolithic period and was occupied by humans between 8,400 and 8,000 years ago. Archaeological evidence shows the site was wooded and that Mesolithic people were using the area close to a small river during the summer months to take advantage of local food resources.

Stone Age flint knapper

© Winchester City Council

Discovering a lost world

Archaeologists have been working on the site since 2000. The work has focused on recording and recovering the Mesolithic material that is constantly eroding out of the seabed due to natural processes.

Artefacts recovered to date include examples of worked wood that have been preserved by the soft silt of the Solent for thousands of years. Of the flint pieces discovered on the site, more than 40 are struck flakes in a remarkably good and sharp condition. Close study of these flint tools reveals that they were made with the aid of an antler or bone hammer. The waterlogged nature of the site has preserved evidence which is unique in the UK, making this a site of international importance.

Recovering material from submerged prehistoric sites can be challenging. Limited visibility, tides, currents and restrictions on the time divers can stay under water has necessitated the development of efficient excavation methods. At Bouldnor Cliff an innovative method of bringing sections of the seabed to the surface was used. Custom-built stainless steel trays enable sections of seabed to be brought up by the diver for further study on land. On the surface, the contents of the steel trays can be excavated by archaeologists with the help of volunteers, allowing local residents to be involved in the excavation of this 8000 year old underwater site.

Volunteers excavating sections of the seabed

3. Yarmouth

Public footpath: The Coastal Path.

Directions: The site can be seen from anywhere in the park to the east of Yarmouth, follow the Coastal Path east from Yarmouth or west from Newtown.

Wikitude: Point your device towards the sea, or choose from the list and select **HWTMA 3. Yarmouth Roads.**

Podcast: Download **Sunken Secrets 3. Yarmouth Roads.**

Yarmouth Roads protected wreck site

Less than 200m from the shore of Yarmouth, at a depth of around 6m, the remains of an important historic vessel are buried in the seabed. The wreck was found in 1984 and excavated during the late 1980s. This work revealed that substantial timbers survive beneath the seabed, especially from the stern of the vessel.

Substantial timbers revealed during excavation of the Yarmouth Roads site

© Isle of Wight Council Heritage Service

The probable date of the wreck has been gained from a range of artefacts that have been recovered from the site. These include 15 pieces of pewter which, along with numerous ceramics, have all been dated to the 16th century.

The ship was around thirty metres long, a substantial size for a 16th century vessel. No definite identity has been confirmed for the wreck, although extensive historic research has revealed a petition in the High Court of Admiralty Records dating from 1567. In this, a Spanish merchant called Antonio de Gwarras sought from the Captain of the Isle of Wight, Sir Edward Horsey, the return of wool salvaged from the *Santa Lucia*. The ship was sailing to Flanders when it wrecked *"thwart of Yarmouthe"*.

The Yarmouth Roads wreck is one of fewer than 70 protected wrecks around the UK that have been designated under the *Protection of Wrecks Act* (read more about protected wrecks on page 25). The wreck site is marked with a yellow buoy that indicates that diving, fishing and anchoring is forbidden on the site in order to protect the remains of the ship.

The Yarmouth Roads site was designated due to the rarity and archaeological significance of the remains. The artefacts from the site provide a rare and important insight into the cargo and personal effects that might be carried on a ship of this era. The remains of the wooden hull provide valuable information about ship construction and the types of vessels used for merchant trade during the late 16th and early 17th century.

Bone comb found on the Yarmouth Roads Wreck

© Isle of Wight Council Heritage Service

As the project funding for excavation of the Yarmouth Roads site came to an end, the site was covered with sand bags for protection and the artefacts deposited with the Isle of Wight Museum Service. The site is now regularly monitored to ensure its stability. With further study the Yarmouth Roads site has the potential to provide more fascinating insights into our maritime past.

4. Alum Bay

Public footpath: The Coastal Path.

Directions: If there is an opportunity, climb or take the chairlift down to the bay. If not; view the site from the talking telescope platform.

Wikitude: Point your device towards the sea, or choose from the list and select **HWTMA 4. Alum Bay.**

Podcast: Download **Sunken Secrets 4. Alum Bay.**

Hidden shipwrecks in Alum Bay
Alum Bay provides the first sheltered area from South Westerly winds after passing the treacherous Needles, where many ships have been wrecked over the centuries. As a result, remains from a number of vessels have accumulated in the bay.

Archaeologist moored over ship remains in Alum Bay

Part of HMS *Pomone*? (Alum Bay Wreck I)

A section of ship, thought to be part of HMS *Pomone* which wrecked in 1811, has been under investigation by archaeologists since 1993. The remains have not been conclusively identified, but recent finds point towards them being part of this early 19th century naval vessel: HMS *Pomone* wrecked on The Needles (see chapter 5), which is a protected wreck site. Here, archaeological investigation has uncovered many artefacts related to the vessel.

HMS *Pomone* was a fifth rate, 38 gun Royal Navy frigate, launched in 1805. It had a distinguished career during the Napoleonic Wars, where it primarily saw service in the Mediterranean.

In October 1811 the ship was returning from the Mediterranean. On board was the British Ambassador to Persia and several Arab stallions; a gift from the Saha of Persia to King George III. Unfortunately in the fading light and October mist, the captain mistook the lighthouse at The Needles for the light at Hurst Castle and the ship hit Goose Rock at the edge of The Needles and was wrecked. Fortunately the crew were saved that night and were able to return the following day to rescue the horses and salvage all the valuables from the wrecked ship.

Archaeological work on Alum Bay Wreck I has included excavation, revealing a well preserved section of ship's hull buried in the sand. These hull remains are around 20 metres long and show a number of ship hull fixtures and fittings. One of the key aims for the excavation was to compare the ship structure and associated fittings in Alum Bay with those from the main wreck site of HMS *Pomone* on The Needles, where organic remains did not survive. Though not proven beyond doubt, it seems likely that the ship remains buried in Alum Bay are in fact part of HMS *Pomone*. Having such a large section of hull in Alum Bay brings a significant new element to our knowledge and understanding of the HMS *Pomone* site.

Diver investigating hawse hole on Alum Bay wreck 1

© Mike Pitts

Other wreckage and finds

Over the years a number of searches have taken place in the bay to map out other interesting finds in the area. Not far from the section of HMS *Pomone*, another wreck lies on the seabed. The visible remains are only about 12 metres long. The identity of this wreck is still a mystery; historical research has failed to uncover any likely candidates for the vessel's identity. As with all archaeology, a vital clue to the ship's identity may still lay hidden on or in the seabed, yet to be discovered.

Another find, a wooden wheel, which appears to be a gun carriage wheel was discovered and recovered by a sport diving group on the area to the south west of Alum Bay. An initial assessment of the wood type was undertaken and showed that the species of wood is an exotic hard wood. The wheel is now on display at the Underwater Archaeology Centre, Fort Victoria, Isle of Wight.

Hurst Castle

Fort Victoria

YAR

TOTLAND

FRESHWA

Alum Bay

4 P

5

6 P

FRESHWA

Freshwater
Bay

The Needles

MILES
KMS

0   1   2   3

0   1   2   3   4

Idnor

A 3054

SHALFLEET

NEWTOWN

BRIGHSTONE

Chilton
Chine

SHORWELL

A 3055

Whale
Chine

te location of wrecks

5. The Needles

Public footpath: The Coastal Path.

➡ Directions: The best place to appreciate The Needles is from the viewpoint next to The Needles New Battery and Rocket Testing Site.

🕐 Wikitude: Point your device towards The Needles, or choose from the list and select **HWTMA 5. The Needles.**

Podcast: Download **Sunken Secrets 5. The Needles.**

The Needles Lighthouse
Guarding the western entrance to the Solent, The Needles occupy an important strategic position.

Unfortunately, they have always been a risky area and a hazard for many ships. The first lighthouse to protect seafarers was erected in 1786 and was placed on top of a cliff overhanging Scratchell's Bay. The lighthouse on the outermost rock was completed in 1859 and still stands there today. The last lighthouse-keeper left this lighthouse in 1994 when it was automated.

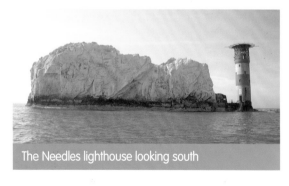
The Needles lighthouse looking south

Over the last 15,000 years rising sea levels have eroded the chalk ridge that once ran from the Isle of Wight through Christchurch Bay to the Dorset coast. This process has left chalk stacks, such as The Needles, as well as the remains of eroded and collapsed stacks, some of which lie as hazards just below the water. Chalk gullies dominate this underwater landscape; some of them are several metres deep.

The Needles protected wreck site

The Needles protected wreck site covers an area with a 200 metre radius (12500m²). The protected area contains the remains of numerous wrecks, of which two have been identified so far. One of them is HMS *Pomone* (see chapter 4), the other is HMS *Assurance*.

HMS *Assurance*

HMS *Assurance* was a fifth rate, 44 gun warship launched in 1747. Assurance spent most of its career in the region of the Spanish-American colonies.

On the 24th April 1753, HMS *Assurance* was returning from Jamaica with the retiring Governor of the island, Edward Trelawny, on board when it ran into The Needles. The ship's Master David Patterson claimed that the ship had hit uncharted rock but was still held responsible for the accident and sent to prison for three months. After the accident the Admiralty was so concerned about the unknown rock that they ordered a survey of the Needles Channel but no rock was found.

Coins found on the HMS *Assurance* site

Another theory concerning why the ship foundered on The Needles can be found in a quote from the 18th century historian John Charnock, who wrote about the incident. It appears that the Governor Edward Trelawny had spoken to the Master David Patterson when passing The Needles:

"He asked a question, suggested by mere curiosity, what depth of water there were around it and how near the ship would pass to that part of the rock appearing above the water. Patterson answered; they should pass so close that the fly of the ensign might touch the rock"

Perhaps the Master's attempt to replicate the boldness of his statement cost him his ship.

6. Freshwater Bay

Public footpath: Coastal Path.

Directions: The Coastal Path goes past Freshwater Bay. Pause here to enjoy the view over the bay.

Wikitude: Point your device out from the bay towards the sea, or choose from the list and select **HWTMA 6. Freshwater Bay**.

Podcast: Download **Sunken Secrets 6. Freshwater Bay**.

Freshwater Bay
The area around Freshwater Bay contains numerous archaeological finds that indicate human settlement throughout history. Artefacts from the Stone Age and Bronze Age illustrate the prehistoric use of the area, while items from the Roman period have also been discovered. Evidence for more recent history and human activity is revealed by a number of underwater finds in the vicinity of Freshwater, notably two shipwrecks recently investigated by HWTMA.

Freshwater Bay

Shipwrecks in the area
Even though the west coast of the Isle of Wight is an area where navigation is complicated, a hazardous environment is not always the reason for a ship sinking.

SS *Azemmour* 1918
About 15 miles offshore in Freshwater Bay a First World War shipwreck lies on the seabed. The SS *Azemmour* was a steel freighter built in 1909; it was used on Mediterranean shipping routes prior to the war.

On the 20th March 1918, the *Azemmour* was on its way from London to Nantes, France, when it was attacked by a U-Boat (UB-59) just south of The Needles. *Azemmour* tried to escape but a torpedo hit the ship's port quarter. The damage was severe and the crew were ordered to get in the lifeboats – there was not even time to return fire. Of the 28 crew members on board, five were reported missing after the incident.

The wreck site now lies 40 metres below the surface and was investigated by archaeologists over the summer of 2010 as a part of the A2S project (see page 25). Despite the passage of time since the vessel sank, it has stayed relatively intact. The ship was recorded as carrying 716 tons of general cargo and 500 tons of steel. The cargo of steel pipes can still be seen stacked in the forward holds, along with several other items that were presumably part of the general cargo. The 90mm stern gun is also visible aft of the engines. The 2010 dive enabled archaeologists to confirm the position, extent, stability and character of the wreck which will inform future management of the site.

SS *Coquetdale* 1940

Another interesting wreck in the area is a Second World War ship, the SS *Coquetdale*. It was a British, steel screw steamship built in 1923.

SS *Coquetdale* was bound for the Clyde as part of a convoy, but was attacked by German 'Stuka' Dive Bombers just off the Isle of Wight. British Hurricanes tried to defend the ships but the sheer number of German aircraft overwhelmed the British and *Coquetdale* was hit by several bombs. The engine room quickly filled with water and the aft deck gun was blown apart. Several bombs hit amidships which blew out the whole port side.

The vessel sank soon afterwards, although the entire crew survived and only two were wounded. The other five vessels in the convoy were all badly damaged.

Top of the piston on the wreck of SS *Coquetdale*

© Dave Robbins

Today, the wreck site is a popular dive site for recreational divers but has also been studied by archaeologists who were able to confirm that the hull of the ship is still relatively intact. However, amidships the hull plates on the starboard side are peeled open, testament to the violence of the explosions that sank the vessel. At the stern, close to the propeller, the hull plates have fallen away from the vessel on the starboard side.

Further work by archaeologists will provide updated information about these two sites and how best to manage our relatively recent underwater heritage.

7. Chilton Chine

Public footpath: The Coastal Path.

Directions: At Chilton Chine the Coastal Path goes inland around the car park. Take the opportunity to look out to sea before the path briefly leaves the coast.

Wikitude: Point your device towards the sea, or choose from the list and select **HWTMA 7. Chilton Chine.**

Podcast: Download **Sunken Secrets 7. Chilton Chine.**

Looking out from Chilton Chine visitors can see an area where several ships have wrecked in the past, some as a result of weather conditions and others as a consequence of human error.

Saxmundham 1888
A 19th century wreck that met its destiny south of the Isle of Wight was the *Saxmundham*. En-route from New York to Stettin in Poland, the iron steam ship was struck by the Norwegian barque *Nor* on Sunday 4th November, 1888.

Harry Saderberg, a survivor, reported that he had been steering west by south before he was relieved at 0200. Approximately ten minutes later a light was seen and shortly after, the *Nor* struck the *Saxmundham* on the starboard side with such force that the ship filled with water instantly. The crew, many of whom had been asleep below decks, began to lower the jolly boat and lifeboat on the starboard side. Several crew members, including Captain Milne, boarded these boats. However the ship was listing heavily as the remaining men tried to launch the port boats which had to be abandoned as the vessel sank.

A curious conger eel on the *Saxmundham*

© Dave Robbins

Saxmundham sank around ten minutes later and the two life boats were able to pick up five more men from the water. Hails to the *Nor* went unanswered and the two vessels drifted apart in the night. On board the lifeboat the eight crew members had to bail out water with their boots. Just before daybreak they sighted a steamer but it failed to notice them. Instead they were picked up by the *Waterbird* which took them to Portland. The jolly boat was also picked up and its occupants were landed at Millwall in London. In all, 12 crew members were lost.

The remains now rest at a depth of 40 metres on sandy seabed that constantly shifts, so that at times it can cover or expose large parts of the wreck. There is a great amount of scattered material across the site and in the middle of the wreck the two large boilers are still standing proud of the seabed.

SS *Joannis Millas* 1896
Joannis Millas lies resting among the gullies off Chilton in only 6 to 8 metres of water, about half a mile offshore. The story behind the wreckage dates to 1896, when the *Joannis Millas*, on its way to Rotterdam, ran aground in mist and darkness and became wedged on the rocks. The ship's forward compartments started to fill with water but there was still hope that the ship could be floated free of the rocks by removing the cargo. Three days later the attempts had proven

unsuccessful and after removing stores, fittings and equipment, the ship was abandoned and considered a total loss.

An archaeologist working on SS *Joannis Millas*

On the site today, boilers, engines and the propeller shaft are still visible. Studying these large iron ships gives archaeologists valuable information about wrecking processes and possible future underwater heritage management issues.

Warwick Deeping 1940
Warwick Deeping, built in 1934, was commissioned into the Royal Navy as an anti-submarine vessel and became another casualty of the Second World War.

On the 11th of October 1940 *Warwick Deeping* was patrolling the south coast of the Isle of Wight together with the vessel *Listrac* when they were attacked by German torpedo boats. *Warwick Deeping* was struck by two shells; one disabled the forward gun, the other hit the ship below the waterline.

The confusion on board was immense, even more so because the crews wrongly identified the enemy vessels as friendly destroyers. Thinking that there would be time to beach on the Isle of Wight, *Warwick Deeping* steered north, but the ship was so badly damaged that the crew had to abandon ship and it sank during the night. *Listrac* was also badly damaged and sank not far from *Warwick Deeping*.

Both *Warwick Deeping* and *Listrac* are popular dive sites for the local dive community. *Warwick Deeping* lies upright and is still remarkably intact.

8. Whale Chine

Public footpath: The Coastal Path.

Directions: Follow the Coastal Path around Whale Chine. The best viewpoint is on the east side of the cliff.

Wikitude: Point your device towards the sea, or choose from the list and select **HWTMA 8. Whale Chine.**

Podcast: Download **Sunken secrets 8. Whale Chine.**

This stretch of coastline along the cliffs has always presented a danger to maritime traffic. In particular, the reduced visibility that results from sailing at night or during fog can be very dangerous. Two examples from the area show how disorientating fog and darkness can be to sailors and how such conditions can result in shipwreck.

SS *Cormorant* 1886
SS *Cormorant* left New Orleans for Bremerhaven, Germany, in November 1886. The ship carried a cargo of cotton. When passing the Isle of Wight, thick fog prevailed and the ship ran aground just outside Whale Chine.

Cormorant beached at Whale Chine

© Blackgang Museum

It was initially hoped that the ship could be re-floated, even though it had grounded at high water, so the cargo of cotton bales was removed and dragged up the cliff by horses. As the weather got worse and the wind picked up to gale force, the ship swung broadside to the beach, ending up on its starboard side. The towboats could not work in the severe conditions and after salvaging what could be removed, the ship was abandoned.

During the *Cormorant's* first night aground an extraordinary thing happened. As if to add insult to injury, an unidentified vessel, having also lost its bearings in the thick fog, drove straight into SS *Cormorant's* starboard side. Such was the force of the collision that the un-named ship left its figurehead on the deck of the *Cormorant* before backing away!

Evidence emerged at the Court of Enquiry that the *Cormorant's* compasses had been out by 11° and no depth soundings had been taken, despite the poor visibility. As a result the Captain was suspended for six months for reckless conduct and losing a valuable ship.

The remains of the ship now lie in about 6 metres of water and are sometimes visible just outside Whale Chine at low tide.

Smyrna 1888

The Clipper *Smyrna* left London en-route to Sydney, Australia in 1888. Good winds gave it a head start through the English Channel but thick fog came down after the ship passed St Catherine's Point. Also in the area was the steamer *Moto* which was on its way from Bilbao, Spain, to Newcastle when it also came across the misty conditions.

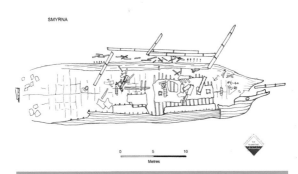

SMYRNA

0   5   10
Metres

Drawing of the wrecked *Smyrna*

The captain and the chief mate on board *Moto* saw the clipper *Smyrna* in full sail getting closer, they gave signal and eventually stopped the ship but the collision was inevitable. *Moto* hit *Smyrna* and tore a great hole in its side. *Smyrna* sank immediately; it was said in less than four minutes.

Of the 28 people that were on board, 12 lost their lives. The Board of Trade agreed that *Moto* was entirely at fault in the incident and a considerable sum of money had to be paid by way of compensation to the owners of *Smyrna*.

Smyrna now lies in 55 metres of water. The wreck was investigated by archaeologists as part of the A2S project (see below) in 2010. The assessment showed that the *Smyrna* is in remarkable condition considering its age, with relatively vulnerable features still remaining, such as deadeyes, bottles and crockery.

Additional information:

Atlas of the 2 Seas (A2S)
Some of the material in this booklet has been collected as part of the A2S project. The A2S project involves archaeologists, students and volunteers from England, France and Belgium working together to research, investigate, survey and promote underwater sites within the southern

North Sea and the English Channel. The project partners are the Hampshire and Wight Trust for Maritime Archaeology (UK), the Association for the Development of Maritime Archaeological Research (ADRAMAR) and the Flemish Heritage Institute (VIOE). Funding for the A2S project has been provided by the European Regional Development Fund (ERDF) through the INTERREG IVA 2 Seas Programme. Further information at:
www.atlas2seas.eu

Protected wreck sites

The Protection of Wrecks Act (1973) allows the Government to designate a wreck to prevent uncontrolled interference. Designated sites are identified as being likely to contain the remains of a vessel, or its contents, which are of historical, artistic or archaeological importance (English Heritage 2010). Further information:
www.english-heritage.org.uk

Primary sources

Wendes, D. 2006. *South Coast Shipwrecks off East Dorset and Wight 1870-1979.*

English Heritage - PastScape (www.pastscape.org.uk/)

HWTMA internal reports

For opening times:

Alum Bay: **www.theneedles.co.uk**

Needles Battery: **www.theneedlesbattery.org.uk**

Underwater Archaeology Centre, Fort Victoria:
www.underwaterarchaeologycentre.co.uk

For more information please visit:
www.hwtma.org.uk

The waters around the Isle of Wight are rich with
archaeological remains reflecting human activity from
prehistory to more modern times. This booklet helps the
reader discover more about these forgotten remains and aims
to give a broad overview of the sunken secrets of the west
coast of the Isle of Wight.

ISBN 978-0-9566224-3-3

9 780956 622433

Published by the West Wight
Landscape Partnership.

**Produced by the Hampshire and
Wight Trust for Maritime Archaeology**

**Tel: 02380 593290
Email: info@hwtma.org.uk
or visit: www.hwtma.org.uk**

Room W1/95, National Oceanography Centre,
Empress Dock, Southampton. SO14 3ZH.

**The Trust is supported by the
West Wight Landscape Partnership**

**Tel: 01983 759779
Email: info@wwlp.co.uk
or visit: www.wwlp.co.uk**

Madeira House, Avenue Road,
Freshwater, Isle of Wight PO40 9UU.